Let's chat about your body & privacy

Written by Nur Choudhury
Illustrations by Jennifer Pacuma
www.involvedfathers.com

Your body is special!

Some parts of your body everyone can

see like your hands and face, while

other parts are hidden and only for

you, they're your private parts.

Page 2

Your body is amazing!

It gives you natural warning signs when

it senses danger or fear or when

something doesn't seem right.

Can you name some signs your body

gives you when it senses danger or

fear?

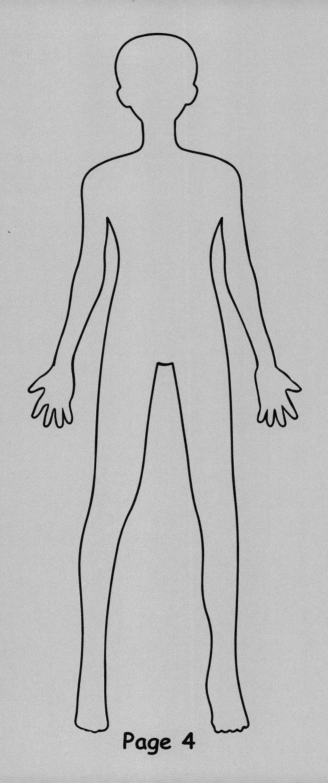

Page 4

You should listen to your body and act in the right way. What should you do when you feel unsafe or in danger?

You should identify trusted adults you can talk to. This is called your 'SAFETY NETWORK' and can include your parents, grandparents, teacher, neighbour, aunt or uncle, coach or doctor.

Identify your 'SAFETY NETWORK'. Name an adult you can trust for each finger of your hand.

It's always good to check with your parents or guardian to confirm the adults you identified are ones you can trust.

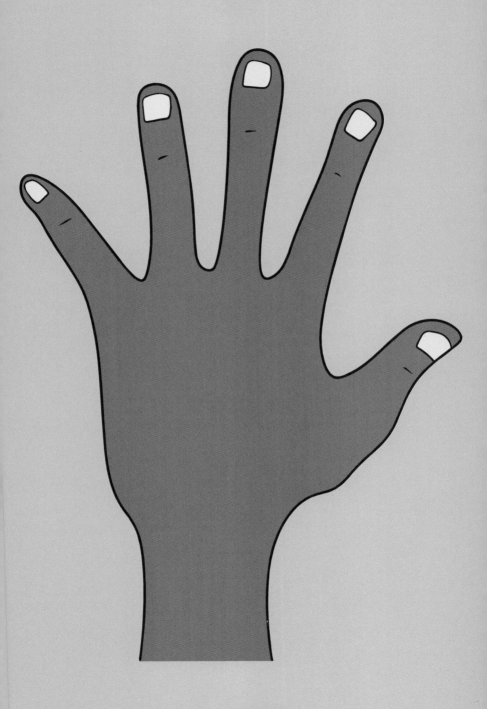

Page 8

However, if you're in a situation where you can't find, speak or contact your 'SAFETY NETWORK' then try and find another adult who you feel is safe or trustworthy.

Look at the image, can you identify an adult you might approach for help if you were feeling unsafe or in danger?

If a situation arises where you feel unsafe or in danger related to your body or private parts, we call this a 'RED FLAG' situation.

Can you help David and Hanna do the right thing as they go through some 'RED FLAG' situations?

Page 12

David is on the bus going home from school and someone dares him to pull down his trousers and underwear for £10.

Hanna gets a message on her phone and laptop asking her to send some pictures of her private parts, the message says that all kids her age do it.

Say?
No

Do?
Put the phone or laptop down and get mum or dad to help report and block the person.

David is at his friend's house and his friend's older brother asks him to watch a video of naked people. The older brother says that everyone watches stuff like this and he's weird if he doesn't.

There are many other situations that you might encounter that are 'RED FLAGS', so remember the following:

1
Your body belongs to you.

2
Your private parts are private and should never be shown to anyone.

3
Listen to your body's natural reactions to dangerous or uncomfortable situations.

4
Know who is in your 'SAFETY NETWORK' and talk to them.

5
Be alert to 'RED FLAG' situations.

FOLLOW ON QUESTIONS FOR PARENTS, CARERS, AND TEACHERS TO ASK OR DISCUSS.

CAN YOU THINK OF OTHER 'RED FLAG' SITUATIONS YOU MAY ENCOUNTER?

WHAT SHOULD YOU DO IF YOU SAW OR RECEIVED A PICTURE OF ANOTHER CHILD FROM YOUR SCHOOL SHOWING THEIR PRIVATE PARTS?

IS IT OK FOR AN ADULT TO JOKE WITH YOU ABOUT PRIVATE PARTS AND WHY?

Printed in Poland
by Amazon Fulfillment
Poland Sp. z o.o., Wrocław

61003597R00016